A Larrikin in the Blood

Also by Michele Fermanis-Winward
and published by Ginninderra Press

Threading Raindrops
The Eucalypt Distillery
To the Dam (Pocket Poets)
The Sail Weaver (Pocket Poets)
Curdled Milk (Pocket Poets)

Michele Fermanis-Winward
A Larrikin in the Blood

Dedication

To my uncle David Owen whose father, also David Owen,
was Tilly's grandson

A Larrikin in the Blood
ISBN 978 1 76041 992 9
Copyright © text Michele Fermanis-Winward 2020
Cover image: Michele Fermanis-Winward

First published 2020 by
GINNINDERRA PRESS
PO Box 3461 Port Adelaide 5015 Australia
www.ginninderrapress.com.au

Contents

Introduction		7
1	Sarah Newman/Avery, The Power House, Hampshire, England	11
2	Jane Avery, Of Men and Rushes, Hampshire, England	31
3	Mary Ann Dann/Avery, The Firebrand, Dublin, Ireland	51
4	Matilda Fellows/Avery, From Threepenny Upright to a Pound a Week, Soho, London	99
5	Emily Whitbread/Duncan/Avery, Where There's a Will, Fingal, North-west Van Diemen's Land	125
6	Matilda Avery/Edwards, Rewriting History, Hobart	143
Timeline		161
Acknowledgements		163

Introduction

For the English, the eighteenth and early nineteenth centuries were a time of social upheaval and foreign wars, of Highland clearances, transportation and slavery. They witnessed the start of the Industrial Revolution, the appearance of non-conformist churches and the emancipation of Catholics.

They also saw the emergence of humanitarian causes, of secret brotherhoods and the forerunners of unions. The French Revolution inspired uprisings across Britain and elsewhere; England lost its American colonies. The Napoleonic wars resulted in food shortages and embargoes. The eighteenth century ended with the United Irishmen uprising of 1798.

To thwart French interests in the area, England wished to establish a colony close to Bass Strait, near modern-day Sorrento in Victoria. My four times great-grandfather, John Avery, was a convict in that attempt of 1803. It failed, due in part to the poor soil and lack of running water. For England, there was little economic advantage in the site, no suitable timber for shipbuilding and no coal for its factories. England deemed the continent to be uninhabited, with no regard for the peoples who had thrived in its conditions for millennia. When the Van Diemen's Land colony was faced with starvation, they did not learn from the local people but waited for supplies to come by sea.

John Avery was a labourer from South Stoneham in Hampshire, aged twenty-four with a wife and young child when he was arrested for stealing a grey mare. This was a hanging offence in 1802 and he had been in gaol before. Horse theft was a popular crime of young rural men. The jurors at his trial were chosen from landowners who generally had a poor opinion of the working men before them. The law, its courts, officers and prisons fostered brutality. Theft of goods above twelve pence resulted in the death penalty and there were 220 hanging offences. Some jurors were lenient and devalued the theft to avoid a prisoner being hanged, and most death sentences were commuted to transportation for life. A first offence would not guarantee you were sent to the colonies; women and children were rarely transported on their first or second conviction for petty theft.

From known facts concerning the lives of my forebears, births, deaths, marriages, the dates and places of convictions, I have filled in the gaps between by imagining how I, and by extension they, would react to situations forced upon them and the choices open to them at the time. From a Hampshire village in 1750s England to 1870s Melbourne, a boom town before the 1890s depression, these are the stories of six women. I begin with Sarah, born in 1738 and the mother of convict John Avery, then his two wives, Jane and Mary Ann. I imagine the lives of his son William's two wives, Matilda and Emily. The final story is of William and Matilda's daughter Tilly. Through their eyes, we see the impact of crime and punishment in England and Ireland and the young colony in Van Diemen's Land, how some prosper while others fail. The six women find their own ways to get by.

Like Tilly, who settled in Melbourne's bayside during the 1870s, I lived on the bay in the early 1950s and remember its unmade sandy roads, the dirt man calling and the smell of a full pan in summer. I also recall my years as an inner-city student with lean-to doorless bathrooms tacked onto the rear of houses and toilets down the back by the lane, being scared of who might lurk in the dark. I could hear my father's caution to his son and daughter when we were small and eager to explore, of Spring-Heel Jack who roamed our bluestone lanes with a cut-throat razor in his hand.

There are threads which connect the generations through our stories and traditions, in our features, strengths and short comings. I am grateful to these women for their fortitude, and I celebrate the larrikin in my blood.

1

Sarah Newman/Avery
The Power House
Hampshire, England

Sarah Newman, 1750, aged 12

Family
they sent me out
servant to a farmer's wife
that I may be of use to the smaller girls.

I see them after church
and when we've supped
I school my younger sisters
in skills I'd learnt that week.

I do not share
the lack of sleep or aching back
sharp words my mistress gives
when I do wrong
nor the groping hands of men
who find me in the barn alone
when they will not be caught.

The working lads are full of cheek
it's older men I fear
they persist, cannot be swayed
believe it is their right
to pounce upon a maid
so I must hone my wits.

The mistress sees me flushed and cross
tells me to find a man
with some chance in life
not fond of drink
nor gaming at the inn.
Well, I've no time for that!

I'm out of bed at five
rake fingers through my hair
don cap and morning skirt
splash water on my face
they're all asleep bar me.

I stoke the kitchen fire
and set about their meal
then off to Jessie's byre
her warmth's a comfort in the dark.

I strain the milk
and fill the master's pail
dip my finger in the cream
it's so delicious
perhaps a little more.

The kettle's purring on the hob
a bite of bread and cheese
with half a mug of tea
it soothes me to my toes.

Upstairs I air the beds
clean and set the fires
run down to sweep the floors
prepare two loaves of bread
then out to churn the cream.

Each day the tasks are planned
no time that sets me free
my mistress oversees it all.

The cow is fed, the pigs have swill
grain for the hens and ducks
the goose pecks at my hem
then in to bake the loaves.

*

It's gardening day
I hitch my skirt
so it will not be spoiled
now I can weed and hoe
before the rain returns.

The mistress calls to me
for there is soap to make.

A cauldron in the yard is set
to boil the fat saved for this day
take care it doesn't burn.

We soak fine ash
strain and mix it in
she cautions me that lye
is harsh on skin and clothes.

I stir and skim until it's thick
and the mistress bids me stop
transfer it to a wooden mould
that we can pull apart.

Once cut to blocks
that fit our hands
she lets me choose a piece
a gift from her to my Ma
such a fine new skill I've learnt.

I lock up the fowl
hiss back at master goose
hurry in to change my skirt
and down to lay our meal.

I slice the bread and ham
recall how it was hung and smoked
so I can tell the girls
make sure to store it right
set pickled eggs and onions in a bowl.

I take a slab of cheese
turn rounds we made last week
fetch ale from our brew-shed
while turnips and potatoes boil
the men will soon be home.

The whole is crafted by our hands
I would make a comely wife for any man
one my age and full of life
such as William in the fields
when he is ripe to wed.

I judge him more than handsome
with his thatch of tousled curls
built large and strong
he's taller than my brothers
with a smile that lights his face.

If he can tame the hive
when the bees are in a frenzy
then he shall earn a kiss
plus some honey for his Ma.

1760, aged 22

A few more years of growth
and I supervise the house
no more dirt or chasing after pigs
they trust me with the keys.
It does my family proud.

The master says that William
will not come to much
but he's a steady lad
and I could marry worse
which is a form of praise
for nothing pleases him.

He offers Will a living for my sake
with a cottage down the lane
that needs a bit of care
and some thatching on the roof.

Ma and Pa had hoped for more
but won't stand in our way.
We may wed at harvest festival
when our vicar posts the banns.

While William and his brothers
transform our home to be
limewash and waterproof it
repair the boards that sag
it is thatched like gleaming new.

His mother sews us curtains
spins and knits our counterpane
his sisters make the mattress for our bed.

His father crafts a table
and a settle with a stool
their industry's the tonic
that soothes my parent's fears.

The mistress hosts a party
for all the family and friends.
We have gifts of linen, pots and crocks
I am overjoyed and bustling
in and out the rooms.

Will thanks them all politely
tells me that I should rest
this time on the morrow
I'll be his lady wife.

Sarah Avery, 1766, aged 28

Now I've a household of my own
and a child comes soon enough
the mistress brings my sister
to help me with the work.

You trained her well, the mistress says
I blush with pride and take my chance
beg her leave
they keep me as their chatelaine
when the babe is here.

She laughs and says we'll see
as I waddle up the stairs
to count the napkin store
and check the fires are set.

1774, aged 36

Will does not begrudge
the hours I'm at the house
he knows an extra serve of meat
or pot of ale is his reward
when I return at night.

The mistress says they are well pleased
with all he does for them.

My little ones are hale and fair
they're ready for the dame school
which the mistress kindly funds.

1780, aged 42

Young William is a little wild
and leads the others into folly
especially John who does the most
to earn his brother's praise.

I caught him setting sticks alight
they burnt a hole in our hedge
he gained a second beating
for the lie of blaming someone else.

1800, aged 62

This war with France goes on and on
the price of wheat doubles every year
as the poor amongst us grow.

They subsist on charity
the love of family and friends.

I give what can be spared
and when the harvest fails
good men are forced to poach and thieve.

The courts respond and pinch us more
rob families of their men
as wives and children starve.

They fear a revolution
have seen the French example
believe we plot against the Crown
and want our lords in chains.

The church takes sides
against its common folk, condemns
what need has forced on them
it preaches heaven will reward the meek
a sermon lost beneath cold hunger
stealing round the pews.

Our neighbours now beg alms
turned out of home
they're sallow-eyed with shame.
Poor folk meet the hangman
for the paltry sum they steal
are exiled for a shilling's worth of theft.

I suspect my sons go poaching
for the thrill it gives
as much as aid our kinfolk.

Despite their stealth
I know when lads are not abed
the house feels chill
emptied of their warmth.
It's a risk we can't support.

Even lads well fed like mine
partake in village justice.

A sack of wheat
is stolen from our barn.
Will and John decide
who the thief must be
and steal a pig from them.

I wait for a rap upon my door
told my sons are in the county jail
till a hearing of the court
and judgement of the landed gentry trial.

William tries their patience most
they confine him for a month
and then two more
the charge
a ewe, a pig or goat is lost
there's no proof of his guilt
he has the knack of walking free.

Not so my John
a fool he was to steal that mare
well known to be another's.
They will hang if not transport him
I pray for some reprieve.

I cannot understand
John's reckless disregard
of Jane and small Eliza.

They married soon as it was legal
with no family blessing
we urged them both to wait.

Not bull-headed John
he went off in secret
returned to say they're married.
He is beholden for the care
of his wife and child
now we must take
that burden on ourselves.

John did not learn
the consequence of actions
never wary, too open-hearted
always trusting that his luck would hold.

I ache for loss of him
to know that I will never see
my cheeky boy again.

His father says
the colonies can make a man
give him a life
with land and property
beyond all hope
of prospects here at home.

1804, aged 66

Jane is turning out
better than we thought
she is resourceful
has found a craft
that suits her situation.

Our village and the vicar
are full of praise
for the goods she makes.

Will and Beth prosper at her side
though Beth weaves only ribbons
and she's often poorly.
I fear will end in sorrow for my boy.

I suspect Jane thinks my John
a costly indiscretion.

With her comely looks
silky hair and well turned body
she will have no trouble
finding someone else to wed
though her Eliza may dissuade them.
No man wants another's lamb to feed.

1805, aged 67

At last
a letter from my boy
such relief to know he is alive.
Two years since it was written
I question why
it takes so long to reach us.

John surely worried
when we did not answer.
Must they invent
more cruelty for him?

Dear Mother
We have arrived safely after all
the seasons here are upside down
as days become exceeding hot
there is no stream that we can find.

He writes,
I cannot reason how
they set on this location.

It does not rain
the ground is poor with twisted trees
that have no use for building
their leaves smell strange
and taint the air when crushed.

Settlers spend all day in grievance
to any who will listen
demand some fertile land
without a threat of ambush.
The naturals give us trouble
but we have guns enough.

We shall decamp
sail for Van Diemen's Land.

Do not concern yourself
I am well despite privation
and not as bad as some.

I believe that wayward urge in me
is mastered by the troubles I have known
and hope to earn a grant of land in time.

Give all my blessing
Your loving son
John.
P.S.
There are the oddest animals and birds
the swans are black, not white
at the bottom of the world. J.

2

Jane Avery
Of Men and Rushes
Hampshire, England

Jane Avery, 1802, aged 25

Hulks
rammed against the Portsmouth mud
gulls wheeling overhead
I watch as men in chains
descend into the dark.

Sun warms the hill
where children whoop and shout
my shawl bound tight
I tremble with an icy fear
of all that lies ahead for us.

Our small child at my feet
I bless her ignorance today.

I was too green
and unprepared for love.
I met a lad who filled my heart
believed his fancy words
John claimed to be a yeoman
and I should want for naught.

He wove a future in my head
I know shall never be
all that's left are broken vows
and a child who needs my care.

Ma warned me of his lies
she asked the vicar
who asked another
until the truth was found

he's but a lowly manual
who works another's land.

She said
this union will degrade us
your father, rest his soul
was in a worthy trade
John possesses nothing
but his parents' good repute.

But it was all too late
he had me in a thrall
I only knew
what my heart could hear.

We waited
till the law allowed us wed
we lacked consent
from all who wished us well
bar his eldest brother.

Today I meet his mother
on this vantage point
we stand in vigil for our John
she'll not see us fail
Eliza's all she has of him.

By sheer hard work
I'll prove it's not our fault
John stole that farmer's horse.

Old customs fall from grace
the squire and his men
no longer in accord
dependant on each other
for a living from the land.

We resent the rule of greed
they call us indolent ungrateful sods
set sheep on ground we tilled
that fed whole families
no quarter found on either side.

I blame the rich men hoarding grain
anger builds within the byre and town
to see our foodstuffs shipped away.
There are riots, whispers spread
of a plan to seize the grain
before it leaves our coast.

The Crown is scared we poor
will stir rebellion here.

We all must make our way
a little theft here and there
to fill an empty pot.
Twin lambs are born
the shepherd blames a fox he didn't see
enjoys a meal on his brother's plate.

Candle ends the maid secretes
to light her parents' home
or honey slipped into a pocket pot
these won't be missed.

If the mistress has a gentle heart
she lets you pilfer without cost
mine told me not to be a sneak
but ask for bits they could not use
a dress she had worn out
remade by Ma
it clothed the two of us.

Now on my own
the mistress cannot take me back
her husband says
John's guilt reflects
brings shame upon their house.

Mother says
I must prepare myself for grief
it bides with us all day long
until we know John's fate.

To escape the noose
when asked his trade
John boasts that he's a blacksmith
such skills are wanted in the colonies.

One look could tell
he doesn't have the strength
those lords don't know
a reaper from a smithy.
They will not be pleased
when his lie's found out.

He is exiled
must leave his home for life.

1805, aged 28

John writes
I am to join him when they're settled
it's just another lark to him
how careless he now seems.

Eliza is too small
to risk on foolish plans.

Sailors' wives share tales
of what their husbands saw
a land of empty wilderness
mens' hunger and their drunkenness.

The godless naked naturals
who freely kill with stone-edged spears.

They warn
there are torments men in hulks endure.
John will be starved and beaten
by vicious gaolers
he must waste in chains
have his spirit broken over time.

When he's no more
than a wretched beast
they can send him to the colonies
to slave for England's wealth.

I would not know him then
so altered by the brutal nature of his plight.

I must fend for Eliza and myself
some small place
is where I wish to be
and find a settling of our lives.

His brother William takes us in
Beth his wife
is a loving friend and sister
values what I know for making do.

She likens me to tinkers
repairing scraps that some may toss
I don't take it as offence.

Their village
is far from squabbling gulls
and sailors' raucous cries
Ma's neighbours with pinched brows
sharing cautionary tales.

Here fields are deep in growth
with a scent of cows and sheep
wide meadows and clean air
through the seasons of the earth.

The vicar seeming kind
not fattened on self righteousness
welcomes me to church
speaks of a weekly market
that follows Sunday service
praising all the farmwives
for their industry
and the wares they bring to sell.

I have a notion that may provide
for Eliza and myself.

The skill taught by a sailor's girl
we made usefuls for the home
hearth brooms, small mats and trays
from knotted straw and woven rushes
working side by side
at the water's edge.

Deemed ourselves resourceful
as we hawked them door to door
for the farthings they would bring.

The war has meant embargos
on imported straw
a lack of summer bonnets
the ones I see are looking old and frayed.
Our local reeds and rushes
must do the work instead.

The sun is high and warm
I will attempt a sun hat for Eliza
hope to recall the craft of distant years.

Beth joins me in the rambling
as we gather all the grasses that I need.

At first I find it hard
with many breaks and tangles
my hands are burning in the effort
to control odd lengths and endings

always keeping to the notion
of why it must succeed.

In time
a rhythm can be found
my fingers working nimbly
and the repetition soothing
as I weave and shape
from the crown towards
a patterned flourish on its rim.

When my hat is finished
I sew pink ribbons on the side
a present from dear Beth.

She is twirling round in circles
insists on wearing it all day
propped rakish on her head.

Beth orders one for herself
and another for her Ma
desires I take all
the ribbons she has made
and we can share the profits
when they come.

Will has a lean-to where I store
the makings for my work
and a barrel for their soaking.

As I complete each hat
we hang it in the kitchen
to dry and set its shape.
Beth sews the ribbons
embroiders J and B in a circle
so folk will know our craft.

We will test them Sunday
with our range of sizes
I hope they prosper for us.

To make a bold display
so that all may see our wares
Will crafts a birchwood tripod
we can pull apart with ease.

The day turns warm and bright
as the market fills with people.
Our hats are like a maypole
ribbons flutter in the breeze
some folk come enquiring
as we leave the church
drawn to those we wear.

To our delight we sell
eight of the twelve
have orders promised
in the large and smaller sizes
with some in manly styles
for husbands working out of doors.

Beth will buy the threads
for weaving of their bands.

So pleased we are
with bartering of wares
and the coin collected.
To celebrate we share a joint of pork
and wash it down with ale.

John's Ma is proud of us
suggests we buy a hawker's licence
to stay within the law.

1806, aged 29

I have an introduction to the local mill
they have a girl Eliza's age
know the troubles of our John
and wish to aid us if they can.

The mill race and the pond
have willows, rushes, reeds
prized weavings for my craft
the miller says t'would be a service
to see them put to use.

And so, Will and his brothers
harvest barrowfuls for me
his sisters bundle and I stack
till our lean-to overflows.

I spend my waking hours
weaving mats and hats and scoops
as gifts for all their help.

Now I can pay my way
I write to Ma and to my John
so they may share in our success
take heart for the future.

*

A letter from the colonies
censored by the Crown

John is made an overseer of convicts
writes he feels a traitor
now his friends despise him.

It's difficult to balance
obeying orders
while being lenient as he can.

The rules are harsh
and he must punish all transgressors
the only good is in a larger ration
he would prefer
to be among his hungry men.

Mindful of the censor
John is loath to bare some truths
but I can read what he implies
beneath the crossed out sections.

His men are not so vile as others
some overseers find
bits of flesh lopped from their noses
and whole ears removed
to mark them as betrayers.

I marvel that any can survive
the senseless cruelty
within a hierarchy of villains
John says he tries
to protect the youngest lads
I can only guess
how those boys are used.

John agrees Eliza is too small
for the long sea voyage
and wild nature of their colony
his future is uncertain
he says I am to wait a few more years.

Well, there's no hurry at my end
it sounds a frightful place!

This village holds and supports us
folk see me as a widow
which in law I am.

Our business doing very well
I go to fairs within my range
while Beth sells in the village
on our licence.

Besides the bonnets, we make mats
and little brooms, soft baskets
the odd scoop and trinket
Beth and I are busy all the time.

*

I return one night to find she is abed
Will looking pale and anxious.
Her lungs were never strong
she coughed throughout the winters
and now she is so ill
we must send for the doctor.

He says it is too late
for anything but prayer.

We are in the deepest mourning
poor Will goes to his Ma
while I pack up my things.
It is unseemly
to be here when he returns.

The miller takes us in
has room for all my makings
he says my wares displayed outside
will brighten up the mill.

I have lost my dearest friend
and all the love we shared.

I keenly sense the break
in connection to our John
with him so far
making new affections there
we now must live
a distance from his family.

More work will ease my heart
we need the money it will bring.
Eliza's growing strong
at nearly six years old
the age when I had learnt to weave.

With no parent in the trade
I did not think to follow on
now I have mastery of this craft
Eliza learns from me.

I will teach her ribbon making
for the start.

I cast aside a future life with John
devote myself
to the living we build here.

1810, aged 33

There's a baker calling round
disturbs me at my work
he tries to win my favour
buys the largest things I weave.

The miller says he's kind
and prospers in his trade

I must admit
that baker has a winning laugh
and seems straightforward
says he values all hard work.
Despite my best intentions
his banter leaves me smiling.

But the last man
that I trusted with my heart
stole the best years of my youth
and left me in distress.
I became a widow through his crime.

Eliza has no memory of her father
the pain cuts deep
I am loath to rush that path again.

3

Mary Ann Dann/Avery
The Firebrand
Dublin, Ireland

Mary Ann Dann, 1790, aged 10

I found myself among the orphan poor
where nuns taught us to sew.

My work was delicate and fine
in this I did my best
and so I made vestments for the priest.
Heads bent we chanted prayers
jabbing in and out
along our lengths of cloth.

The younger girls would weep
not for the stab of needle pricks
but for the cane
a speck of blood would bring.

I cursed them all beneath my breath
the nuns who thought a child was trained
by shaming and abuse
that beating was a substitute for love.

We were a parliament of girls
on two competing sides
the Reds and Greens.
Our leaders set the policy
and should a girl transgress
what punishment was apt.

The opposition curried favour
with the holy crows
did all they could to please
informed on our exploits.

We called them bloody knees
for crawling to the nuns.
They called us stinking nettles
for the trouble that we caused.

We plotted and we schemed
found honour in revenge
used sabotage and theft
against the priest and nuns.

Some feigned ignorance
to voice their discontent
it ended with a caning all the same.

The nuns would never lose
but we could make them work
for our pain and tears.

Always clung to one another
for the warmth we craved
found delight and comfort
in the one thing we could offer
the passion of our bodies and our hearts.

1795, aged 15

Now I am sent to work
the household is not grand
but rich enough
to keep a needlehand like me
who can sew and mend all day.

The children sometimes sweet
the cook is mean, the butler sharp
the master and the mistress
not so harsh as others tell.

I am busy with the linen
or in making clothes
and the basket fills with mending
from their family down the street
which increases all the time.

I share a bed with the maid
Kate is bold and full of chat
she has a comely face
of button nose and dimpled chin
with so much flesh to hold
my convent bones dig in and make her yelp.

She loves to tease
it keeps me warm at night
so I'm grieving less for my dearest Greens.

1798, aged 18 – the Uprising

We are crushed by martial law
gangs murder, loot and maim
rape women not in hiding.

The blinds kept drawn
I work by candle all the day
we cannot let them see us
and dare not step outside.

At night I'm making dressings
for our wounded sons
Irish blood pours down the streets
and no excuse is heeded
if a man is found abroad.

Our martyred numbers swell
into their many thousands
while gaols are filled with harmless boys
we pray for our salvation
respite from guns and gallows.

1805, aged 25

We convent girls stay close
share news about our lives.

Molly was abused and ruined
they sent her to the Magdalenes
and there she scrubs and sews.

Tess was widowed by the Protestants
she gets by with help.
Jenny Bow is married
to the footman at her place
so she is set for life.

Now Annie writes her plans succeed
before the court again
that petticoat she stole
gives passage to the colonies
where they are short of wives
and every man can own his land.

What a brave colleen
she turns misfortune to advantage
no matter how unlikely
will prosper in any place she lands.

Always keen to taunt
the Reds would say
a face like yours
would never get a man
even one who's blind
and thrice your age.

I'm not much in that regard
my hair's too black
will not be tamed
no matter how it's tied.

My eyes are blue, deep set
they're lost below thick eyebrows
and I've a nose, a conky beak
larger than is just in a woman.

Freckles swamp my face
with a mouth that's small and thin
my smile is good I'm told
though few may know it.

I dare not test my luck
who knows what choice I'd have.

1810, aged 30

Days stretch into their years
of darning holes and stitching hems
my eyes and fingers swell
but still they keep me on.

Kate has wed, how I miss
the cuddles that we shared
the new maid is a dreary thing
churlish and she snores.

I should not find complaint
no one has sought my heart
the cook has softened though
and I am rounding out.

Annie sends me drawings
of her life in New South Wales
with a farmer who seems kind
and three children in a row
she has servants to command
is urging me to join her.

Some days I feel no more
than a shadow on the wall.

*

There are crowds at Sunday market
noise and jostling on all sides
as I buy a square of cotton
the devil seems to take me
and I palm a coil of ribbon
try looking calm as cheese.

Inside my heart is thumping
and I scurry to the alehouse
to ease my shaking hands

I won't chance that lark again.

For a month I am contrite
sweet as syrup to a fault
but the urge is overwhelming
to feel alive again.

There is danger on my mind
this time I thieve a yard of silk
distract them with my banter.

I smile and thank them nicely
to get myself away
and watch if someone follows
from an alehouse down the lane.

With the thrill and speed of drinking
I am feeling rather giddy.

That night I sew a dainty gown
for Bridie's little one
will post it on the morrow
no one shall guess its taint.

I wallow in my guilt
but sinning is the way of all mankind
part of me is weeping
and part of me is cheering
for the game I'm at.

I press on to ruin
getting bolder at my craft.

I have a choice of bonnets
to shield my nose and hair
but sometimes note suspicion
a narrowing of eyes
when I stop and browse.

I buy a penny ribbon
to put them off my heels
twice I have been followed
adding spice to Sundays out.

I always go to mass
make my confession, light a candle
do penance to St Nicholas
and hope he understands
then totter home a little lost in drink
to the best sleep of my week.

*

I did not see him watching
nor that he followed me
I felt his arm pull roughly at my basket
expose the stolen reels.

Here in the Dublin gaol
we are a motley group
from the poorest lass in rags
to on the town and fancy girls.
There are ladies just like me.

Our gaoler is a brute
she reminds me of the nuns.

Patriots here say English laws
are keeping us enslaved
every act against the Crown
is for our martyrs' sake.
We should all take heart
and cause the English trouble.

*

A month I stayed
was helped by Jane and Kat
they are loving friends in that special way
both know the tricks for getting by
in here and on the streets
how money can be made
to fund a jolly time.

I have no trouble finding work
despite the piecework pittance
they toss me a penny
charge their customers a shilling.
I work fast and neat
can thank the nuns for that.

1813, aged 33

Twice more I've been inside the cells
am feeling quite at home
with my old companions here
who are more than dear to me.

We are a merry crowd
that sing and dance at night
we trade our skills and barter
have wine and spirits
the finest fare to eat.

Most ladies ask the magistrate
send me to the colonies
where it is always warm
and there is hope for everyone.

I like it here
but Annie begs me join her
I'll have a chance this time.

*

On board we have to wait
in cold and wet for months
no bedding or warm clothes.

The war with France holds us back
waiting for a convoy.
I can only dream
of the comforts back in gaol.

The voyage is a horror
with waves that send us reeling
and gaolers who parade
the jaws of fearsome sharks
just to see us cringe and weep.

The fairest of our ladies
are sent to be the playthings
of the officers and men.
By age and disposition
I am saved from that distress.

We dose them with a physic
so they'll not land in ruin
at the port of New South Wales.

Annie is to meet us on the wharf
I will be her 'servant'
till I find my way along.

At last we are arriving
I give thanks to Mother Mary
we survived that great ordeal.
Here's my dearest Annie waving up at me.

There seems to be confusion
with the papers she provides
and I am marched straight past her
to the female factory.

The Governor's decided
he needs us in Van Diemen's Land.

There is nothing we can alter
but I feel my spirit breaking
at the loss of all our plans
and my uncertain future
without the aid of friends.

Once more I'm shipped away
and naught but to endure it.

We sail south against the wind
are then blown further north
it takes us many months
to reach our final point.

A year aboard these creaking hells
we trust no more to see.

1814, aged 34 – Van Diemen's Land

We talk
easy by his side
on the path to his house

says he picked me from the rest
because I seemed not meek
nor too wild
and I'm of his age.
Well, he looks somewhat older
and he's turning grey!

He sensed I hid a rebel in my breast
but did not think it showed.

He desires to be a yeoman
I protest, knowing little of the land.
John says his work at home
was in the fields and seasonal
the skills of kitchen farming
were his mother's craft.

She knew more than all of them
the care of hens and pigs
of brewing and small dairy work.

Instead of learning at her hem
he ran behind his brothers
found mischief by their side.

A woman in the yard
is what he needs the most
feels adrift without the sense
that women seem to bring.

John talks to me of Jane
and all the hurt he caused.
His Eliza's almost grown
but letters rarely come.

His house is small and dry
the cook house where I sleep
is mine to order as I wish
and there's a patch of land
for me to garden.

I learn how fruit and fowl
work together in the soil
what weeds are good to eat
and where to forage.
I trade my sewing skills
with the neighbour wives.

How I miss the company of women
beside me in the house
but John is kind
with a gentle manner
I've not met in other men.

While he's out at work
I grow vegetables we need
learn why some may sprout
when others wilt
and how to prune a rose.
I am filled with pride.

The blessings tumble in
I'm pleased to be assigned
to such a cheery man.

We share stories of our time
as prisoners of the Crown
of torments in the hulls
and his sympathy for the Irish cause.

I tell him of the heartbreak
caused to me and Annie
ask if she may visit.
Anytime, he says.

He jokes my cooking skills
need to be refined
but I'm a willing worker all the same.

We make do when tea and flour
or sugar can't be found
and meat is scarce or strange.
I do not take to wild meats
he brings home to cook.

John says
when the colony was starving
men were kept alive
by boiling washed-up blubber
with seaweed scrapings off the beach.

It sounds a useful poultice
for a skin rash not as food.

Now he asks
will I share his bed
a compliment to one as plain as me.

I know the pleasures of my body
but feared how it would be
in bed beside a man
not sure if I should move
or respond to what he does.

The nuns had always said
it was a loathsome act
but wives must submit
we should pray to Blessed Mary
for the child it brings.

I had presumed his weight
bearing down on me
would be excessive
to have his flesh inside my body
as painful and repellent.

I'm surprised
it's more pleasure than my girls
thought fair to mention
and practice makes it better.

I tell him he is scared I'll run away
unless he ties me down
remind him I'm a Catholic.

John secures my permit to be wed
and we plant a rambler rose
to celebrate our union.

Knopwood is a drunken fop
but there's no priest bar him.

Mary Ann Avery, 1815, aged 35

Before the year is out we have a son
the nuns were right about that pain.

John names him William
for his elder brother.
He is beautiful like a cherub
my colouring but everything
in perfect balance for a boy.

I never thought such riches
would be mine.

1816, aged 36

I take in sewing
from the Ladies on the Hill
beside my skill at needlework
they've heard I'm open-minded.

I stitch their fancy garters
and lace bodices
finest muslin undershifts as well.

I try one on for size
John is amazed
how sheer the fabric is
afraid to touch me
till it is removed.

1818, aged 38

John has a grant of land
he's been working there alone
now he wants me with him
but I'm happy to stay here.

He thinks that husbandry
is but a simple art.
I suspect there's more to pasture
than mere sun and rain.

I have learnt to compromise
overcome my doubts
believe this man
tempered by the convict life
knows best how to proceed.

With my support his plans
will prosper in the end.

I must leave our cosy house
say good bye to my friends
in Red Lantern Street
the Ladies on the Hill.

I can no longer sew
the latest mode for them
loose drawers in silk
some with lace-edged slits.
Their customers love a novelty.

John doubts their taste
says it's such a dainty thing
needing extra care
and getting in the way
be there a slit or not.

The Ladies spoil my Will
as we leave
his pockets bulge with sweets.

They laugh and say
when you're grown make sure
you learn to please a girl
come back sometime
but on your own, young Will.

I am laughing too
to think I once sewed for the priests
and now my skills
have earned us whorehouse coin.

I confess with all the gardening
and in keeping house
my sewing is no longer fine.
My eyes are oft-times sore
as I stitch our rough farm clothing.

We load a cart
take the north road to John's land.
Close to the Derwent ferry
his plot adjoins a bay
he named it Green Point farm
and here we pitch our tent.

I line the floor with rushes
while John collects large stones
to weigh our canvas in a wind
and surround the cooking fire.

I meet the neighbour wives
who come with gifts
an apple tree and rose bush
bearing hips all ripe for pickling.

John snares a swan to roast
while I hear about the soil
how to defend
a kitchen garden in the wild.

*

And now the season turns
from the warmth of autumn days
working by John's side
I am forced to seek my shelter.
There is constant rain and sleet.

We are living in a mire
I fear for baby William
insist we leave
before his chills get worse.

We will return in spring
or when our home improves.
John sets to building pens for sheep
and a sturdy hut for us.

1819, aged 39

Life on the land is hard
I ache most days
but life is good to us
we have three sons
William, Edward for my Da
and now there's baby John.

I watch my husband bent at work
sometimes see him rise and stretch
take in the river and his land.
The soil is poorer that we hoped
our plot is small and full of stones.

While he is tall and strong
we need a man to help
in grubbing rocks and roots
then we can plant a crop.

Within two months
we have a lad to help.

Ted is seventeen
was in the cobbler's trade
but fell to stealing lead
and has ended here with us.

He seems a kindly lad
I intend to care for him
as any mother would.

John wants a larger patch
it will see us bound in debt
he plans a legacy for our sons.
I fear he has not learnt
what a farmer needs
to prosper in this land.

Good health is not enough
you need goodwill and luck
to be in favour with the gentry here
and you need a ruthless heart
not pushed aside at your first stop.

I will not dash his plans
John's open heart trusts easily
perhaps I am too harsh.

*

The best of our new farm
is the beautiful timber house
with room for all of us
and privy out the back
plus a sturdy barn.

The kitchen garden's fenced
so wildlife can't get in
they cursed my days at Green Point farm
swans and ducks ruined all my work.

Sheep and cows can be penned
but those birds
were more than clever
always finding points of weakness.
Will did his best to shoo them
bellowed when they pecked.

We lease the Hobart house
hope to clear our debts in advance
but I fear that John
may overreach himself.

Our new farm sits
within a nest of vipers, the ex-marines
who meted out their cruelty
kept John in fear
aboard the ship *Calcutta*
and in our colony's first years.

They will never call us friends
despise all convicts.
I must presume they wish us ill.

Should we run foul of them
their ranks would close
tighter than the chains
John endured back then.

1821, aged 41

Another son for us
he looks a little odd to me.

His face is flat with eyes the shape
of one who's from the East.
John thinks he will come good with care
but I'm past forty now
and weary in my bones.

There is grudging respect
from our neighbours here.
We have discharged
the debt upon our farm
and there are three young men
who work the land with us.

With child again, it seems we prosper
but my legs and ankles swell
till I can barely walk
needing help with all my tasks
and the flies get into everything.

It breaks my heart this baby comes
a month before it's due.

After troubles with our George
I doubt that it will live.

At last a little girl for me
she is a perfect dolly
but very small and frail.
We call her Jane, for our friend
and in respect for John's first wife.

She and George take all my time
he is slow and often ill
needs oil rubs for his skin
and steam to aid his breathing
but he is loving to a fault
always eager to be my help
a thing I sorely need.

His brothers bait and treat him rough
George loves them more for it.

His speech unclear
despite the time we take to listen
he loves to talk
so I must learn some patience.

As I nurse our tiny Jane
and supervise the lad
that works our kitchen garden
my eldest two, Will and Ned
are schooled at Mr Gray's.

1823, aged 43

John is taken for sheep stealing
protests he was deceived by others.
That I can believe!
Swears he bought them in good faith.

There's a witness says
John knew full well
they were not clean.

Whether he was bribed
to speak against us I can't tell.
He might hold a grudge against my John
from something in their past
or he's just hoping for improvement.

We know free settlers scheme
to rid the land of us grant holders
but surely we no longer fit that class.
Our land was open market bought
and paid for with interest.

Perhaps that reckless streak
John could never tame
and his trust in other men
has led to our undoing.

He may have been less sure
of where those sheep came from
and could not pass a bargain.

1825, aged 45

I'm half mad with grief and rage
my baby girl has died.
John sentenced fourteen years
sails for the Gates of Hell
and black Macquarie Harbour.

From stories that we hear
he will be flogged and worked to death
in constant wet or eaten when asleep
by his neighbour.
I doubt he can survive

Outside the courts
I thrash young Ned for getting in a fight
beat my darling son until he bleeds.

I'm sent before a magistrate
time in the factory to repent
weep for the harm I caused my boy
for all the hope that's lost.

Our land and goods, our home
are forfeit to the Crown.

Poor Ned is taken from my care
trained by the orphan home
to be a docile servant
just like his Ma.

Johnnie with our friends
is helping on their farm
they treat him like their own.

Will looks big and strong for a lad of ten
gets his keep as stable boy
for Mr Page's coaches
and George, unaware of our plight
is staying close by me.

He giggles at the games
others play on him.
I give thanks to Mother Mary
all my boys are roofed and fed.

They set me down
to make the convict drabs
these slops are all I'm fit to sew.

Most stitchery is beyond me now
my fingers stiff and bent
from farm and garden work.

I can't see to thread a needle any more
a useless bag of bones is what I feel.

They shear me like a ewe
to show the town
I am beneath them all
it fuels the bile in me.

If I'm to be a beggar on the street
I will look them in the eye
and not be cowed.

I laugh as George tries to paste
the locks back on my head.

*

John's petitions are ignored
our pleas for mercy are denied.

My audience with the Governor was unwise
doubt I showed the level of humility
to his office or the Crown.
The cruel bastard was too busy
stringing up more hapless souls
and hunting natives down.

I'm in the direst poverty
must seek the aid of friends,
how else is George to live
he has no understanding
bar the hunger that he feels.

They call me a whore
because I'm keeping house
for the man who worked for John
as I did before when mistress of our home.

Ted is not inclined
to a worn out rag like me.
He courts a youngster for his bed.

In the town at night
my George asleep and safe
I get drunk, weeping in my gin
telling friends the cruelty of it all
until my grief is numbed.

Loss is more than sorrow
it cleaves the mind in two.

I find myself at the watch house door
bold enough to shout abuse
until they round me up
and toss me in a cell.

The bench calls me incorrigible
sets the usual fine
five shillings I don't have.

This is an awful place
both men and women venal
the law was never one
to use its power for good.

Lawyers dispossess smallholders
the same plot sold in England
New South Wales and here.

Three owners fight for one possession
the titles and surveying
take years to disentangle.
Bribes stretch boundaries
and fencing comes by whim or prosecution.

Beyond the town
is murder and bushranging.

Troops of men go out
fuelled by hate and rum
with no regard
for all the lives they're taking.
They think it is a game
to kill and rape black women.

Natives have a bounty on their heads
like the tiger skins we see.
Two peoples are divided
by ignorance and fear.

I look back to our uprising
and the host of Irish martyrs
when asking to be free
meant you were slaughtered.

In this colony
of convicts and their masters
where cruelty is the norm
one they see as different
will find no mercy shown.

I lie awake in fear
pray my darling George
should not be left
with no one to protect him.

1828, aged 48

From Macquarie Harbour
John writes
the regime's brutal but he endures.
Says he learns about compassion
two men resolve to end their misery
one kills the other
with a witness there to testify
and see the killer hang.

John complains the leeches bleed them dry
their skin rots in the unrelenting wet
and he is always cold.

The bread is poor and mouldy
but they've found a native tree
with leaves to ease their pain
which are chewed or sometimes smoked.

I must ask him more about them
would be a godsend for us
if it's true
and cheaper than a pot of rum or gin.

He accepts their guards have work to do
and strives to cause no trouble
though the toil is often crippling.

The man is turning soft in the head
perhaps he finds it easy to submit
a thing I never could
but I have not been flogged
and forced to work in chains.

He begs I forgive the harm he caused
but that crime destroyed our lives
and the prospects of our sons
a guilt he'll wear all his days
and his church cannot absolve.

I write
William prospers in his work
no word from his brothers
but I trust the same for them.

Forced so young from my care
all I can do
is pray they meet with kindness
pray they're not misused.

George and I send our love to him.

John teaches
in a hut built just for him
protected by a mighty wall of logs
the wind's a constant worry
sweeps all they do away.

His pupils are the soldiers
and their sons
some favoured convicts who are willing.
What a twist of fortune
because of him
our sons cannot be schooled.

John writes he'll be assigned
to the Reverend Robinson
out New Nolfolk way
swears he'll never test his luck again.

He sounds contrite and beaten
by the whole regime
or maybe
he just feels his years at last.

*

Dear John,
I bide with Will and George
we can visit when you're settled
see how things
might sit between us then.

Will needs a steady rein
sometimes turns bull-headed
reminding me of you
and George is George all the same
wants extra care with his lungs each year.

If the Reverend is willing
he would love to work beside you.

John is free to care for us again
still proclaims his innocence.
We survived our deprivations
but I resent the cost to our lives
there is a rift between us now
and he says I coddle George.

1832, aged 52

Will sets his heart on a doubtful choice
one of the Princess Royal girls
she looks frail to me
I can only guess her past
from all my Ladies tell.

Friends at the factory say
she took sickly on the boat
gained no skills they taught
and kept their surgeon busy.

Held by the Orphan Home
not fit to wed or work till now.

She seems a child against Will's bulk
and lacks the strength
one needs to be a wife.

Sent to help the Pages' cook
who took pity on the girl
she can't take heavy work
at least she learns to peel and boil.
It falls to me
I'll show her how a home is kept.

1834, aged 53

John's so pleased that Will is wed
his family gathered round.
It's good to see the light
in his eyes again.

Matilda vexes me
the poor girl has none of her own
apart from the cook
who treated her so well.

I've seen the pox and what it does
suspect Matilda has it.
My Ladies say those Princess Royals
come with doubtful histories.

I'll dose her with some herbs
won't say what they are for
would spoil it all for Will
and she is kind to George.

1836, aged 56

Matilda does not listen
refusing to be told
cooking is the only skill she has.

Her house appears a shambles
with dingy floors and windows
she takes all day at washing
though her clothes look stained to me.

I tried to be a wife to John
but failed and fail again
he loves me still, I can't forgive
the death of my sweet Jane
and the hardship of my boys.

By our link to Sarah Island
we are reviled
deemed the worst of the worst
in the convict class.

I never hoped to be grand
or to rule a house of servants
I just want a kinder life
without abuse from neighbours.

We are despised by the town
they mock my simple George
say he is God's curse
the proof of our bad blood.

Now my darling boy is taken
by congestion of the lungs
he was the dearest soul I ever knew
and the comfort of my heart.

The church expects me humble
to beg with tears and pleading
but I won't grovel
for the charity they offer.

I've done my penance now
and purgatory besides.
To the devil with them all.

1840, aged 60

I make a life on the edge
don't steal, but nudge the law
enjoy my time at the Factory.
It reminds me of old Dublin gaol
with dancing, plays and pantomimes.

There are bullies all the same
who prey on younger girls
I thwart them where I can.
Their threats don't bother me
protected by the Ladies on the Hill
and my age or reputation.

I find comfort with the patriots
Dubliners like me
we buy and sell carved buttons
wear shamrock coloured kerchiefs
to set ourselves apart.

We nurse and care for one another
a family if you like
who accept me as I am.

4

Matilda Fellows/Avery
From Threepenny Upright to a Pound a Week
Soho, London

Matilda Fellows, 1822, aged 14

Fingers turning white with cold
I fumble at my skirts
his weight and rum-rank breath
rough hands groping in the dark.

I watch for the lantern arc to catch us out
the Watch to pounce
and toss me in a cell.
I don't much care for that!

Beside the preaching and rebukes
I'm fed and dosed
carbolic scoured by pinch-faced hags
displayed for bible wives to judge.

Small for my age
more like a child
Dolly says it's what men like
that plus my chestnut hair.

I charge an extra penny
won't be cheated of my worth.
Threepence gets me bread and ale
tobacco for my pipe.

I'll not be bound
to workhouse orphan's choice
jobs a girl with family will not do
the bawdy house or starve.

Last year I tried a housemaid's lot
was daily thrashed
the mistress finding fault
in every trifling act
so bruised and hurt
I ran away to find a friend
who took me to the courts.

The magistrate was fair
he granted me a bed
at the workhouse here
but free to earn my keep
anywhere I choose.

I know my way about the streets
Pa died before my birth
and Ma when I was four.

Handed round by aunts and friends
soon enough
I learn what men can do.

On the town with older girls
who taught me how to earn
how much to give a pimp
and what to hide.

I also learnt
ways to dodge attention
not snared by other women
nor to leave myself exposed.

When a man turns cruel
I'm sharp
poke fingers in his eyes
stick-thin I wriggle free.

They don't expect my strength
or fleetness when I run
back to our workhouse wall
heart thumping in my breast
as though the world should hear.

A bolt hole to our yard
safe in the dark I feel my way
just space enough for me
to come and go unseen.
Avoid those leeches at the gate
who demand a coin to pass.

I've heard girls tell
they'll send us to the colonies
six men to every maid.

We'd learn to cook
spend months upon the sea
taught how to sew and mend.

I could be the mistress of a house
escape the bullies, rules and spies
toss these scrag ends
the men that rule my life and purse.

I could have a man of my own
not one who wished to change me
but treats me as a friend.

I'd promise to become a saint
to bask in sunshine
fill my lungs with air that's sweet
not fetid hand me down
from men breathing in my face.

The charity takes only girls above sixteen
I'll wait the two years more
makes eight in all
on this pox-fed backstreet.

1828, aged 20 – Pentonville Penitentiary

Here I am
now six years on
from workhouse spike
and being on the town
to drudge at Pentonville
waiting for my chance to leave
trying to keep well
on a list bound for the colonies.

I'm penitent
can mouth the words
as well as any tuppence girl.

We're taken off the streets
sewing aprons from old sails.
We scrub them clear of salt
the scent of ocean rising on the suds.

Some stains persist
I cheek with the girls
on what these marks could tell
of battles and wild seas.

The screw hovers at my side
gives me her crooked snarl
chides 'cease your noisy prate'.

My back is sore after just an hour
hands swollen from the task
a break come noon with stew or slops
depending how my work is judged.
It's just another day.

I'm weakened by the pox
so they send me to the bottom of their list
scratch my name out
deemed not fit to sail.

But I will just keep trying
until they tire of keeping me back here.

1832, aged 24 – Van Diemen's Land

I've never seen a sky as blue
nor sun as fierce
the air's so clear and clean
my lungs swell till my buttons strain.

We see queer animals
and painted birds
the water glows from within.

At night the sky is dancing
with waves of coloured light.

But the best of all
what I can scarce believe
is the open space
around each house
and all the room to spread
beyond the town.

1832, aged 24 – At the Orphan Home

I'm standing in a line
not London streets
but still displayed
like cheese in market stalls
for men to sniff and buy.

I will not be pushed
won't wed because
one stands and grins
drops his cloth at my feet
and hopes I'll pick it up.

These half-starved runts
and rejects from road gangs
don't rate a second glance.

*

Today I have an offer
from a mothery dame.
I'm to help her in the kitchen
of a coaching house nearby
I remind her of the daughter
she was forced to leave behind.

We slice and sweat together
serve the family and their men.
I never knew a heart so kind
with her little gifts and hugs
always caring how I am.

I do all there is to please her
for the loving that she gives.

1833, aged 25

I meet a lad who turns my head
with his energy and brawn
six foot against my less than five
he asks if I will walk with him
is younger by six years.

It's no barrier, he says
likes women who aren't green.

He reaches out takes my hand
it disappears within his grasp
and I feel safe
a thing I'd never felt
beside a man before.

I treat him gentle
learn to care
his mother is a papist crone
with a nose to match
but I can manage her.

His father's soft
a worn-out lag
so full of warmth for Will and me.

Matilda Avery, 1840 aged 32

That Mary Ann is a shrew
finds fault with how I cook and mend
and how I clean.

We cannot agree
I prod the fire
to stem the flames
that burn inside of me.

We argue raise our voices
she goes off in a rage
gets drunk then screams abuse
at the law and Crown
at poor John, at Will and me as well.
She ends up in the gaol
it's to spite me I believe.

Will bails her out and pays the fine
she can't live here
of that I am steadfast

I know what it's like
to find yourself alone
having none to guide you
with their caring and support.

Instead of taking me
as a loving daughter
with all the gifts
that bond would bring
she holds me as her rival
baits me where she can
making sympathy the harder.

1842, aged 34

Eight years without a child
cursed for the life I led
they die within my womb
and months of sickness
I can't hide.

His mother
brews her hideous weeds
I choke them down
or bring them up
without a change of fortune.

This time
I'm feeling hopeful
as the baby grows inside me
I am stronger than before
and may hold it to full term.

I sob with the relief
so tired and weak besides
feel as though
I've given birth to a foal.

William sings and laughs
holds his newborn son
the babe seems strong
cries lustfully
and I have milk enough.

His mother coos
even smiles at me
brings hot rum and butter
which is better than her tea.

1844, aged 36

Mary Ann is knocking at our door
Will lets her in
she no longer calls
when he is out of town.

She's lost her mad Flash Mob
at the Cascades Factory.

Most are dispersed by now
but the remnants
are tighter than before
and those Ladies on the Hill
give her a bed
handouts and hand me downs
from the mercy in their hearts.

No longer fit to work
she does a little trade
in pretty buttons.
I thank her for the set
she brings our Tilly.

I suspect
she's found the peace
she lacked since John was charged
and left them wanting.

After tea with a dash of gin
she flounces off
in her whorehouse dress
always wears that bright green kerchief
it's the badge of her Factory lot.

1848, aged 40

Will can be restive
grieves for his Ma
could not see her faults
how often she was drunk
and abused us all.

She warned against the reckless vein
in his father and her son
though she was
the wildest of them all.

Will needs a bigger life
coaching gives him room to stretch
the mastery of beasts at speed
it has the power he craves.

I note the flush on him
when passengers admire his style.

He relives his escapades
of dodging gangs and rutted tracks
to see his charges safely home
and warm inside the inn.

George cannot bear to stay behind
so eager to be like him.

My sickness comes as fits
to wake or slumber through
some days it hurts to think
with thoughts askew
words stumbling from my mouth
but children must be fed
though it wears me out.

Will dotes on George
and takes him in the coach
if he is granted space.

Tilly helps me where she can
potters in the yard
grows vegetables
taught by her Pop.
She is the nurse to me
helps cook and sweep
when I can barely stand.

1850, aged 42

John comes to live with us
the poor man is so aged
by the troubles of his life.

All that he owned
worked these years to reclaim
now lost to other hands.

He could never make it right
for Mary Ann or their boys.

He is penniless like her
but she was stubborn
with a self-destructive pride
that would spark
if she was crossed.

We sit and talk
of how things were at home
my time in London as a child
his life upon a Hampshire farm.

Mary Ann would tell him
of her Dublin days
and brushes with the law.

I filter mine
describe the smog
ripe market smells of cheese and fish
the din from peddlers
and the barrowmen.

He talks of Jane
his first love and their Elizabeth
how they made straw goods
did very well
at fairs and market towns
until the end of war with France.

They could not compete
when the imports flooded back.
Jane re-wed
a baker he believes
and Eliza has a healthy brood
lives in Hampshire still.

His two boys Ned and Johnnie
are somewhere on the diggings
Bendigo he thinks
we've not heard any news of them.

He sighs
says the only thing
to show for all his years
is Will and I and our two.
He thanks me for the kindness.

I reach for his hand and squeeze it
reassure him
his being here does me a service
such a tired and shrunken
dear old thing he is.

Tilly dances in
shows us her bowl of peas
so proud of their harvest
she gives him a hug
sits at his feet to pod them.

He is a patient tutor
as she counts them out
and spells the names
of other things they've planted
he writes them on a slate
for her to copy.

With tea, a pipe and company
the burden of my illness
feels a great deal lighter.

1855, aged 47 – Launceston

We move to this odd place
of bible preaching hounds
I feel hemmed in and alone
no friends beside my Tilly.

George at work with his dad
I miss old John the more
the flavour and brash colour
of my godless Hobart Town.

1862, aged 54

Will is charged with furious driving
a year and I've not seen him
don't really blame the man
I am past desire for pleasure.

I've had suspicions in the past
who knows how many tots
are his without the name
between Hobart and Launceston?

Tilly fumes.
I warn the wind may change
and stamp her face
with Mary Ann's temper.

She feels injustice keenly
insists her dad does right by me
says the women of this family
have been wronged enough.

*

We go before the court
Tilly insists
we should appear
in our oldest clothing.

I mumble at the judge
cannot raise my head
feeling ragged and ashamed
next to Will
who's looking very fine.

We are granted a good living
enough for both of us
if we don't get above our station.

5

Emily Whitbread/Duncan/Avery
Where There's a Will
Fingal, North-west
Van Diemen's Land

Emily Whitbread, 1854, aged 17

He sells me like a keg of beer
to save himself from ruin.

Ma's entreaties go unheeded
I dreamt of someone dashing
a young man full of passion
who would sweep me out of here

but Pa commands I wed
this dried-out shopkeeper.

I weep for the waste
of my youth and beauty
upon a dour and greying
tight-pursed Scotsman.

Emily Duncan, 1856, aged 19

James demands I sweep and scour
then help him in the store
my friends are never welcome.

When I complain he says
I'm young and should do more
or gives a curse
and strikes my face in answer.

Worst of all he's plain in bed
a thrust and grunt
then he turns and snores
I'd hoped for some attention.

Despite his schemes
Pa finds that he is bankrupt
and James controls the inn.

I won't have Ma's assistance
she would always bring me gifts
tried to ease my chains
now I must endure
the old brute's meanness.

I'm so bored by this place
a backblock village
with only sealers for amusement
or the Company men
their talk is full of sheep and cattle
or how much land they've cleared.

When the traders visit
show me samples from their range
they tell me of the Town
its shops and bright attractions.

I order from their catalogues
feel smart in my new clothes
then see I'm out of date
in the fabric or the cut
or the colour of my gloves.

With our children born
James is a little kinder
gives me space to mother them
no longer at his heel
between inn and hateful store.

I have time to read again
though I hide this fact from him
he only reads his paper and the Bible.

Friends slip me books unseen
if I can't have the life I wish
there are lovers and adventure
inside these penny bloods.

1858, aged 21

I know that I am pretty
men tell me so
not handsome like the gentry
who look so grand in weekly papers
but I can make lads blush
when I catch them staring.

The coach from Town
comes twice a week
and it overnights at our inn.

I chat to William who's the driver
he's a favourite here
a big and bold, very friendly man.

While James is out the back
I tell him of the books I like to read
he laughs, makes out he's shocked
and says he'll find
more scandalous ones for me.

We start a little caper
William telling James
there's a ladies' magazine
that he could bring for me.

It's much admired by the Town
filled with homely, practical advice
and in return I can pack him lunch.

James browses through its pages
says improvement in his home
would be appreciated, adds
I have a lot to learn.

Despite its sober tone
the magazine is welcome
a useful guide to all things modern.

Ma says we need diversions
from the roughness of our lives.

James is pleased
to see the change in my demeanour
and soon with each edition
a novella hides, read and returned
in William's basket with his lunch.

But things are getting better
it starts with a squeeze
as we pass in the hallway
a kiss on the back of my neck
sends a shiver through me.

When James is at lodge meetings
we tumble into bed.

He fondles me
and every hair responds
I pulse between my legs
am helpless groaning
as his tongue and teeth lick-nibble
from my toes up to my head.

The touch of his calloused hands
that tug on reins all day
and gently tickle me at night
in places he likes moist.

Agile as a stallion
he guides me to his member
I wrap my legs about him
gasping breathless at his pumping
he stays himself until
we both erupt with pleasure.

I can barely find the strength
but am back into our rooms
deep asleep on James' return.

All week I feel the memory
of his body and its heat.

The maid suspects
says his sheets are stained and twisted
the towel beneath us useless.
She declares he has a woman
or if not, then he indulges
that large appetite himself.

I tell her, let the poor man be
his wife at home is mad
and we won't speak to James
of the little sport
William and some local tart might have.

On Ma's next visit, without a word
she can tell I have a lover
gives me a knowing smile
says she hopes I'm sleeping better.

1860, aged 23

We are planning my escape
quiet as a moth I pack
goods I could not bear to lose
my silver brush and ivory combs
a fine embroidered shawl
gifts to me from Ma
and dainty things a woman needs.
I hide my bag in the store.

How I long to end this subterfuge
as my belly swells, is it James'
or is it Will's?

The pains begin
how long and hard
this child takes to be born.

James is a stringy man
with sandy hair
our children taking after him
including his grey eyes
I hope this one takes after me.

This babe is large
with eyes of piercing blue
and a mop of coal-black hair.
It's the colouring of Will's mum
the Irish showing through.

James comes in to see his son
then yells abuse at me
despite my fragile state
he lashes out, cuts my mouth
gives me a bleeding nose.

The midwife says
she's sending for the constable
if he lifts his hand again.

James disowns the child
so I name him John
after William's dad.

Next time the coach departs
Will has me and baby John inside.

I can live in a proper town
won't need to pretend
he's just another man at the inn.

1861, aged 24

James advertises
he won't be held responsible
for my debts, says I deserted him
without just cause
years of bruises give a lie to that.

He tells the world
the babe I nurse does not belong to him
he would not search for me
and there is no reward.

Will and I have a room
in the house with his son George
we romp and lark every night he's home
I doubt large towns
have time for village gossip
here I'm just a woman in the crowd.

Will's daughter Tilly
says she will not shame herself
nor dignify my abandoned state
by coming to our home.

She sends George with threats
from her to Will
demands he pays for their upkeep
or she's taking him to court.

At times I must admit
there's something dark
that's held inside of Will.

He goes silent, looking grim
only horses raced at speed
will change his countenance.
Perhaps it's their disgrace
at the convict crime of John
a restive need, despite the risk
to test himself again and again
never quiet in his soul.

He will bolt head first
free his coach from bog or ditch
strain himself
but never ask for aid.

Now a summons from the courts.

Before the magistrate
and displayed to gain his pity
Matilda looks an imbecile.

Tilly pleads, this pathetic invalid
takes all her time and care.
Would his Honour see them starve
in rags, begging at church doors
while William has employment
dressed in coachman's livery
of top hat and finest coat
with good money he can spare.

A pound a week!
The magistrate's been duped
I could live on half of what she gets
Tilly's old enough to take in washing
provide for all their wants.

That Pentonville whore
is bleeding William dry
and we have little ones to feed.

Emily Avery, 1865, aged 28

While she met a cruel end
I could not wish on anyone
at last we're free to marry.
No more sniggers about bolters
or reproving looks our way
when another child is born.

1868, aged 31

How proud I am
the town agog with royal patronage
my William in control
of Mr Page's greys.
Prince Alfred close beside him
taught to drive a coach and four.

When the dignitaries are ready
Will hands his reins to the prince
and off they trot at pace
Hobart to Launceston
George drives behind them
with the Governor's wife and ladies.

The paper's there
with a photographer
to show the world how grand
Will and George appear
in their new red coats and top hats
the harness and the horses
all polished to a gloss.

We'll be waiting at Town Hall
with flags, a band and bunting
to cheer when they arrive.
It's a pity Till's not here.

1870, aged 33

Now settled and with children
Till has softened.
She brings her brood
to see their Pop
tells Will he works too hard
should leave the heavy lifting
chides he is no longer young
despite the baby in his arms.

Till admires the watch
with the Prince's coat of arms
a gift from him to Will
she read about it in their paper.

As they nurse our little girls
she thinks it quaint
her kids have aunts
younger than themselves.

Her Bill has just enough
to buy a plot of land
says he'll build the house
a few years on
or maybe speculate.

He works for men
who buy ten-acre lots
then subdivide, build and sell
growing all the time
sounds good
so long as there's no downturn.

I know how soon a rich man
can turn into a bankrupt
and the gold
won't last forever.

6

Matilda Avery/Edwards
Rewriting History
Hobart

'Tilly', 1850, aged 6

Mum and Pop
are chatting in the yard.

Pop and I dig and plant together
peas and beans and flowers
the roses are my favourite
I love their size and perfume.

Pop tells me
Nan loved them best as well.
Mum scoffs
it must have been the thorns she liked
then says to Pop she's sorry
for words against the dead.

Pop says I look like just her
in my colouring and eyes
but without her nose
which Mum says is a godsend.

My Pop is very old and bent
his skin is brown and wrinkled
he lives with us, helps Mum
to lift and carry, she isn't very strong.

Some children spit when I pass
and hold their noses.

They call me convict spawn
tell their friends I'm dirty and dishonest.
Mum says best to ignore them
but their taunts hurt all the same.

I love to be outdoors
feel the air upon my skin
the wind howling through the trees
I can listen to the birds
and know them by their calls.

I can't go off and ramble
like my brother George.
Dad says there are bushrangers
who capture girls like me.

If I am very good
and Mr Page allows it
Dad takes me on his coach
rugged up I sit beside him.

Pop says I'll pass the farm
he and Nan once owned
marks it on a map drawn just for me.

Not far from town
I point towards a bay
that's filled with swans and ducks.

Dad says he loved it too
but don't tell Pop
would only make him sad.
Back then he says
birds were everywhere
and fierce as well.

Nan would often cook young swans
for Sunday dinner
said it was revenge
for all the mess they caused.

Dad tells me names
of towns that we are passing
mountains and the rivers
what birds we see
there's some I've not seen before.

We love to watch black cockatoos
admire each loping wingbeat
with a call that sounds so strange.

Dad says the story Nan was told
is they are murdered natives
it's why there are so many
crying for their fate.
Nan would never harm one.

When it's time to break our journey
rest the horses at an inn
I have fruit, custard and jelly
that is layered in a glass.

1855, aged 11 – Launceston

It's a special treat for me
today I work with Dad and George
Mum says that she's well enough
still I fear to leave her
so a neighbour will look in.

We're in the stables at first light
a smell of hay, harness and manure
horses eager to be out
restless in their stalls
steam rising from our mouths
as I greet each one by name.

My favourite is the grey
I steal a mouthful of her oats
munch as I comb
brush her till she shines
though I can't reach to her back.

We spread new hay
the old piled in a heap to age
clean manure has a separate mound.
George will spade it into sacks
place it in a handcart by the gate.
Dad says every tuppence helps.

George, his apprenticeship begun
will drive a coach between the towns
when master of the reins.

I am called into the kitchen
fetch a mug of tea for Dad
and milk with bread and jam for us.

I like our new home here
there aren't as many bullies.
Mum says that she is lost
without her old familiars round.

Here we don't have history
I'm not afraid of gossip on the street
from lags begging at our door
reminding us of the past.

All the same, I miss my Pop
we're told convicts are wicked men
especially one like him
doing wrong again
but he was the gentlest man
would help anyone who asked.

Dad says it broke Pop's heart
to lose the farm he loved.

When it came onto the market
despite us having money
that topped the asking price
Pop never had a chance
they were set against him.

Dad says that fancy dealing
was at work again.

1861, aged 17

Mum is deserted by our Dad
he lives with Emily bold as you like
a tart who thinks she's grand
because her father built an inn
and gave her name to it.

She's just a bolter like my dad
and her mother was a convict.

I pity the old fool
she flatters and deceives him
Dad thinks he hasn't aged
will push himself to prove it.

George still visits once a week
but backs Dad's side
gives a little where he can
says Mum is too far gone
to be of use to anyone.

I can't take work outside the house
she needs my help with everything
always anxious when I leave her.

I grow enough for soup
it's all she wants.

Now, with nothing left to sell
we are forced to seek assistance
from the courts
must be exposed
to another bloody scandal
Dad's brought on us.

Mum cannot speak on her behalf
she sits there looking tragic
while I plead our case.

Bloody Emily's there
scowling down at us
dolled up like a strumpet.

Well a pound is all we get
for the bother and the gossip.
I know people at the church
are whispering about us.

Always small
today Mum looks more shrunken
spends her time
neither worse nor better
prodding at the fire
and all her waking hours
under my or George's supervision.

He comes most Saturdays
so I can get to market.

I don't let her near the pot
especially when it's boiling
but in a trice she overturns
soup that I was heating.

I sit her on the bed
wrench that bloody poker from her hand
tell her to stay till I return
and shut the door behind me.

I run into the neighbours
ask if they have milk to spare.

Three minutes gone
and I return to horror
finding Mum alight
her dress and hair in cinders.

I throw a blanket round her
she is calm and unaware
as if the flames were just a breeze
that's passing by.

Her skin so burnt and raw
no hair, it breaks my heart.

The guilt increases
when wounds become infected
poor Mum has lockjaw now.
A pain so bad her last days
are worse than any hell I could imagine.

Mum finds release
though it was truly wretched
I hope she finds a gentler place
by the fire in heaven
where she can prod for all eternity.

George is contrite, says
he should have served her better.

Tell that to our dad
the bloody mongrel would not pay
for extra care
or the medicines she needed.

1864, aged 20

I go out to work
char to a lady from our church
well there's no hardship cleaning house.

I meet Bill, their handyman
bricklaying's his profession
he gardens on the side
while saving all he can
plans to settle in Port Phillip.

We are open with each other
with no jokes or cruel asides.
He invites me to a meal
no fancy place I say
I don't have clothes
for anywhere but our local.

How easy are my days
without dear Mum to watch.

I must put aside my scruples
taking Bill to meet with Dad
the law requires his blessing
if we are to be wed
and he should meet the cost.

How Emily will be crowing
to see me at her door.

Matilda Edwards, 1866, aged 22

I am married to a steady man
who has a useful trade
but shall I never cut from our history.

The gossip wears me down
our name has notoriety
they talk of Nan as if she was
the leader of a bloody gang
not some destitute, drunk old lag
that Mum was fond to claim.

This town knows all about
the court case against Dad
with a pittance for our keep
and the shame of Mum's demise
hoping there's more scandal.

Always happy to amuse themselves
at our expense.

Behind it all is Pop's conviction here
he was called the sort of names
no man should call another.

1870, aged 26, Melbourne

We take our leave
board the steampacket to Sandridge.

Melbourners are rich with gold
and building men are in demand
we'll leave the sorry tales behind
and start our lives anew.

No more slurs or being told
my kids will have bad blood.

Bill finds work straight away
and we rent a house nearby
well, half the house is ours.
The man who owns it
says he'll cut the rent
if I can cook and clean for him.

There's a lean-to wash-house
with tin bath
and bricked in copper
plus a dirt can out the back.

Old Dave's reminding me of Pop
a battler who has seen hard times
he finds it tough with just one arm
lopped when he tried to free
a jammed machine at work.

Bill can clear the yard
which is overgrown with brambles
I can't get near the line
to hang our washing.
Who know what lurks
beneath years of neglect.

I tell the kids to play out front
and on the street
till Dad sees to the yard
and don't go down the beach
where the gypsies have their camp.

I add a little to my caution
warn they like small children
will throw them off the pier
as bait for catching sharks.

Wind across the bay
blows sand through every crack
we shake it from our clothes at night.
There are swamps and stinks
from works along the bend.

The kids are settled into school
now I want to plant a garden
grow fresh food for us.

Unlike at home, this land is flat
with sand instead of earth
just like Pop would often tell
of his time Sorrento way
before they built the colony
in Van Diemen's Land.

How they struggled to survive
the heat, the flies and sharks
cruel for men in chains.

He said a few marines were vicious
especially with their own
they would flog a man until
he'd never work again.

Pop remembered lightning strikes
and the bush engulfed in flames
snakes and goannas crowded on the beach
with women and their children
wailing in despair.

He thought the camp
and all they had for their survival
would then be lost.

Men worked in a frenzy
filling canvas buckets from the sea.

As the convicts sweated
ankle deep in sand
it chafed their skin till raw
and salt water made things worse.

We no longer have to sink
holey barrels in the ground
for every drop of water that we need.

Pop said it was so brackish
that men preferred to thirst.

Still I grieve for my good soil.
Cuttings of the flowers I love
wilt and die within a week
things I grew with ease at home
even beans won't take root
only brambles thrive.

We get manure from the dairy
and from the dirt man's horse
I use scraps from the grocer
every little helps.
By degrees
I'll turn this sand to healthy soil
and know abundance here.

Tell the world
there are no convicts in my family.
No larrikins in our blood.

Timeline

1737 William Avery born to Robert and Mary Avery, Hampshire, England
1738 Sarah Newman born to John and Elizabeth Newman
1765 William Avery and Sarah Newman marry
1766 William (Will) Avery jnr born to William and Sarah Avery
1770 Elizabeth (Beth) Binham born
1777 John Avery born to William and Sarah Avery
1777 Jane Wallis born to John and Elizabeth Wallis
1780 Mary Ann Dann born to Edward and Margaret Dann, Dublin, Ireland
1783 England loses the American colonies
1790 Elizabeth Binham and William Avery marry
1793 War with France begins
1798 United Irishmen Rebellion
1798 Jane Wallis and John Avery marry
1799 Elizabeth (Eliza) Avery born to John and Jane Avery
1800 Act of Union, England and Ireland
1802 War with France ends
1802 John Avery convicted, Southampton, horse stealing (death sentence commuted to life transportation)
1803 Colony attempt at Sullivan Bay (now Sorrento, Victoria)
1803 War with France begins again
1804 Establishment of Hobart colony, Sullivans Cove, Van Diemen's Land
1809 Matilda Fellows born to Thomas and Anne Fellows, Soho, London
1813 Mary Ann Dann convicted, Dublin, petty theft (sentence seven years transportation)

1815 War with France ends
1815 Mary Ann Dann and John Avery, marry, Hobart
1815 William (Will) Avery born to John and Mary Ann Avery
1817 Edward Avery born to John and Mary Ann Avery
1819 John Avery jnr born to John and Mary Ann Avery
1821 George Avery born to John and Mary Ann Avery
1823 Jane Avery born/died, daughter of John and Mary Ann Avery
1824 John Avery convicted, Hobart, sheep stealing (sentence fourteen years Macquarie Harbour)
1824 Child of John and Mary Ann Avery born/died
1826 Mary Ann convicted, Hobart, 'inhumanely treating a child' (sentenced to Female Factory)
1833 Marriage William Avery and Matilda Fellows
1836 George Avery, son of John and Mary Ann Avery, dies aged fifteen
1837 Emily Whitbread born to John and Eliza Whitbread
1842 George Avery born to William and Matilda Avery
1844 Matilda (Tilly) Avery born to William and Matilda Avery
1847 Mary Ann (Dann) Avery dies aged sixty-seven
1854 James Duncan and Emily Whitbread marry
1851 John Avery dies aged seventy-four
1853 The last convict ship to Van Diemen's Land
1855 Van Diemen's Land renamed Tasmania
1861 John Duncan born to William Avery and Emily Duncan
1864 Matilda (Fellows) Avery dies aged fifty-five
1865 William Avery aged fifty and Emily (Whitbread) Duncan marry
1865 William (Bill) Edwards and Matilda (Tilly) Avery marry
1871 William Avery dies (from a hernia) aged fifty-six
1880–1900 Melbourne's land boom and bust

Acknowledgements

In researching how my forebears may have responded to the personal, political and cultural events in their lives, I was assisted by numerous works of serious scholarship. Any errors and omissions are entirely mine.

I offer my heartfelt thanks to these historians: Alison Alexander, *Tasmania's Convicts*; Simon Barnard, *A–Z of Convicts in Van Diemen's Land*; James Boyce, *Van Diemen's Land*; Ian Brand, *Sarah Island*; Nicholas Clements, *The Black War;* Tim Hunter, *John Avery*; Richard Cotter, *Voices From Sorrento*; Hans Julen, *The Penal Settlement of Macquarie Harbour*; Hamish Maxwell-Stewart, *Closing Hell's Gates*; Phillip Tardif, *Notorious Strumpets and Dangerous Girls*; Marjorie Tipping, *Convicts Unbound*; Steven Walker, *Enterprise, Risk and Ruin*.

I also wish to thank Gordon Bain; John Bragg; Kiah Davey of The Round Earth Company; Kathy Gerontakos; Peter Ghent, a fellow descendant of John Avery; Vanessa Kiessling; Joy Kitch of the Sorrento Historical Society; and Marie Sedal.

I was able to draw inspiration from three formidable women in my family: my grandmother Isabel (Oakley) Fermanis, my mother Vera (Owen) Fermanis and my mother-in-law Pat (Hamilton) Winward.

I am grateful to my editor Brendan Doyle for his good humour, keen eye and continued encouragement.

Finally, I thank my husband Kevin for the tireless enthusiasm which made this project possible.

www.ingramcontent.com/pod-product-compliance
Lightning Source LLC
Chambersburg PA
CBHW070904080526
44589CB00013B/1181